EnlightenMinds: Journey into the Essence of Education

Preface

Welcome, knowledge explorers, to this timeless journey through the pages of "EnlightenMinds." In a constantly evolving world, education emerges as the golden key that unlocks the doors of learning and enlightenment. This book is an invitation to walk with us along the path of wisdom, to explore the transformative power of education in shaping our past, illuminating our present, and forging our future.

Each chapter is a milestone in this exciting journey, a deep dive into the importance and impact of education on human affairs. From its birth in antiquity to contemporary challenges, we weave a narrative that celebrates the catalytic role of knowledge. Along this path, we encounter enlightened thinkers, bold innovators, and those who have dedicated their lives to bringing the light of education to every corner of the world.

Through the ages, across cultures, "EnlightenMinds" aims to transform education from a mere act of learning into a driving force for change. We tackle the challenges of the present, cast a gaze into the future, and recognize that the power of knowledge resides in each of us. This book is not just a story but a call to action, a hymn to the importance of education as a vehicle for a more enlightened and aware world.

We are all explorers on this endless adventure, and "EnlightenMinds" is the compass that will guide us through the vast territory of knowledge. Take curiosity by the hand and let these pages lead you, for in every word, in every story, there is the promise of a brighter future shaped by the timeless power of education. Welcome to the journey, seekers of knowledge!

Chapter 1: "The Dawn of Education"

Introduction to the History of Human Education:

At the heart of humanity, before the pen touched paper and schoolrooms echoed with youthful voices, education found its beginning in a tapestry of oral narratives. "The Dawn of Education" takes us on a fascinating journey through primordial eras, where wisdom was conveyed through storytelling, songs, and legends. This chapter is an immersion into the very roots of education, a insightful exploration of the earliest flames that illuminated the human mind.

Transition from Oral Knowledge to Formal Education:

Immersed in the darkness of the past, humanity underwent an epochal metamorphosis as knowledge evolved from simple oral transmission to a more structured and formalized method. From dialogues around the fire to the initial rudiments of an alphabet inscribed on stone, this transition is the pulsating heart of our educational history. Exploring the connection between orality and writing, we delve into ancient civilizations that shaped this fundamental change, laying the groundwork for a world where knowledge would be transmitted through codes and books.

Role of Early Schools and Academies in Antiquity:

The early flames of education, fueled by curiosity and a thirst for knowledge, found a home in the schools and academies of antiquity. In this chapter, we traverse the damp courtyards of ancient Greek schools, where philosophers like Plato and Aristotle shared their wisdom with young minds eager to learn. We observe the ancient Roman academies, where rhetoric and liberal arts were at the core of an education that molded the minds of future citizens. Through the dusty words of manuscripts and scrolls, we relive the era when the first educational institutions paved the way for formal education, opening doors to a world of discovery and enlightenment.

The first chapter of "EnlightenMinds: Journey into the Essence of Education" invites the reader to cast a fascinating gaze on how education began its journey, tracing a path winding through stories whispered in ancient nights and the first classrooms that witnessed the birth of the desire to learn. An engaging narrative that lifts the veil on the foundations of human education, laying the groundwork for a deeper and more passionate understanding of our educational past.

Chapter 2: "Illuminating Minds: Revolutionaries of Knowledge"

Introduction to the Era of Great Scientific and Cultural Discoveries:

Our journey into the importance of education now arrives at an era of extraordinary revolutions, both scientific and cultural, a period where minds enlightened by knowledge radically changed the perception of the world. Through the thrilling gateway of the age of great discoveries, this chapter will guide us through the intricacies of a period that left an indelible mark on humanity, an era when minds rose to challenge the darkness of ignorance.

The Influence of Key Figures such as Galileo, Copernicus, and Leonardo da Vinci:

In the heart of this revolution, intellectual giants emerged whose contribution to our understanding of the world cannot be underestimated. Galileo Galilei, with his telescope aimed at the sky, unveiled a previously unknown universe, breaking the chains of scientific dogma. Nicolaus Copernicus, with his heliocentric theory, overturned the geocentric view rooted for centuries. And Leonardo da Vinci, the polymath genius, merged art and science, opening doors to an era where knowledge knew no bounds. We will explore the lives of these revolutionaries of knowledge, peering into the pages of their journals and immersing ourselves in their bold visions, discovering how their ingenuity and determination ignited the flames of knowledge in an age of obscurantism.

Expansion of Universities and the Renaissance:

Parallel to these individual revolutions, the educational landscape was undergoing monumental transformations. The expansion of universities marked an era where knowledge was no longer the privilege of a few but became accessible to anyone reaching out for wisdom. Through the effervescent atmosphere of the Renaissance, where art, science, and philosophy intertwined in a symphonic embrace, the human mind flourished in an endless dance of creativity and discovery. Architects, philosophers, painters, and scientists shared the same stage, contributing to an explosion of knowledge that still shapes our way of thinking and seeing the world today.

The second chapter of "EnlightenMinds: Journey into the Essence of Education" catapults us into an epoch of epic transformations, where knowledge illuminated by visionary revolutionaries opened horizons previously unimaginable. Get ready to immerse yourself in a fresco of bold ideas and unparalleled discoveries, as our journey through the importance of education intertwines with the lives of those who dared to defy conventions and light the path for generations to come.

Chapter 3: "The Age of Industry: Education for Progress"

Impact of Education in the Industrial Era:

In the whirlwind of the industrial age, where the roar of factories merged with the incessant sound of technological advancements, education emerged as a catalytic force for change. This chapter will propel us into the heart of a period of unprecedented upheavals, where education became the key to unlocking the doors of industrial progress. From early mills to assembly lines, we will see how knowledge not only adapted to this new world but shaped it, becoming the primary lever for the evolution of society and the economy.

The Importance of Mass Literacy:

The sound of opening books and pens scratching paper blends with the noise of machines. Mass literacy emerges as the foundation upon which industrialization stands. In a world where written communication becomes crucial, the power of words transforms into an indispensable tool for navigating a rapidly evolving society. We will explore how literacy not only ensured broader access to knowledge but proved to be the lifeblood fueling the engine of innovation and competitiveness.

Growth of Public Schools and Development of Educational Systems:

As factories thrived, public schools multiplied, becoming beacons of hope for emerging generations. In this chapter, we will venture into classrooms illuminated by oil lamps, where teachers became architects of the future. We will see how educational systems developed that went beyond the mere transmission of knowledge, embracing education as a tool to shape characters and minds. Under the guidance of bold reformers, public education evolved into a social catalyst, opening doors to opportunities previously unthinkable for individuals of all social classes.

The third chapter of "EnlightenMinds: Journey into the Essence of Education" transports us to a tumultuous era, where education becomes the currency for industrial progress. On one side, the noise of defining machines of the age, on the other, education rises as the driving force behind the transformation of a rapidly growing society. We are invited to explore the synergy between education and industry, a relationship that has shaped the course of history, opening doors to a future of unprecedented opportunities.

Chapter 4: "Education in the 20th Century: Struggle for Equality"

The Spread of Education in the 20th Century:

The twentieth century, witnessing geopolitical upheavals and extraordinary progress, is also the era when education spreads like a beacon of hope in every corner of the world. Through the tension of global conflicts and the optimism of periods of peace, this chapter of our journey takes us through a map marking the growing presence of classrooms. From industrial metropolises to remote villages, education becomes an increasingly accessible asset, catalyzing social and cultural transformations that reshape the fabric of global societies.

*Civil Rights Movements and
Access to Education:*

In an era where the struggle for civil rights permeates the air, education emerges as a key tool in the battle for equality. We witness freedom marches and the commitment of those who, with courage, challenge injustice. From civil rights movements in the United States to the fight for independence in many parts of the world, education becomes a beacon of hope, a peaceful weapon against the chains of oppression. Through moving testimonies and stories of resistance, we will explore how education has been at the center of a silent yet powerful revolution that changed the face of society.

*The Digital Era and the Evolution
of Teaching Methodologies:*

The advent of the digital era represents another turning point in the history of education. This chapter will guide us through the corridor of technological progress, examining how digitization has shaped teaching methodologies. From early computers to today's portable devices, we will explore how technology has expanded the horizons of learning, bringing classrooms into homes and connecting students across geographical borders. Education becomes increasingly personalized, adapting to individual needs and opening new avenues for learning access.

The fourth chapter of "EnlightenMinds: Journey into the Essence of Education" takes us through the tumultuous 20th century, a period in which education establishes itself as a universal right. From unprecedented dissemination to struggles for equality, to the digital revolution, education reaffirms itself as a guiding beacon for evolving humanity. In a constantly changing world, this is the story of how the fight for education has left an indelible mark on recent history, drawing a path toward a brighter future.

Chapter 5: "The Transformative Role of Education"

Impact of Education on Economic Growth:

In the fifth chapter of our journey, we delve into the deep waters of the economic impact of education. Education is not only a beacon of individual enlightenment but also a powerful driver of economic growth. We explore how educated minds transform into driving forces of innovation, creativity, and productivity. From small entrepreneurs to industry visionaries, we see how knowledge translates into economic development, laying the foundation for flourishing communities and prosperous nations.

The Link between Education and Poverty Reduction:

Through the prism of education, we can observe a radical light in the fight against poverty. We examine how access to education becomes the gateway to a world of opportunities. From rural villages to the heart of metropolises, education emerges as the great equalizer, opening doors once closed and generating a virtuous cycle of improving living conditions. We analyze the stories of those who, with the power of knowledge, have overcome socioeconomic barriers, demonstrating that education is the catalyst for a radical change in wealth distribution.

How Education Contributes to Social and Cultural Progress:

Education is the connective tissue that binds people in a society. In this chapter, we will explore how social and cultural progress is intertwined with education like threads in a tapestry. From cultural manifestations to social reforms, we see how educated minds lead the way toward more inclusive and aware societies. Education is not just a matter of academic knowledge but a vehicle that carries values, worldviews, and critical awareness challenging the status quo.

The fifth chapter of "EnlightenMinds: Journey into the Essence of Education" invites us to probe the uncharted terrain of the transformative impact of education. From engines of economic growth to catalysts in the fight against poverty, to propelling forces of social and cultural progress, education reveals itself as the pulsating heart of sustainable change. Through the stories of individuals and communities, we witness the revolutionary power of

knowledge, carved over centuries
as a bright beacon guiding
humanity toward a future of
shared prosperity.

Chapter 6: "Global Challenges and Educational Responses"

Analysis of Current Challenges in Education:

In the sixth chapter of "EnlightenMinds," we courageously venture into the current landscape where, despite progress, education faces complex challenges. From access disparities to educational inequities, we examine urgent issues that demand our attention. Globalization has brought benefits but has also highlighted significant divides. Through in-depth analysis, we unveil the crucial knots threatening the very fabric of education, from resource shortages to cultural barriers.

Innovative Solutions to Improve Access to Education:

The chapter then shifts to a fertile ground of innovation, exploring bold solutions that seek to break down barriers to education access. From community initiatives to international efforts, we immerse ourselves in the stories of those shaping the future of education. Scholarship programs, online learning networks, and community-integrated educational projects are just a few of the creative and adaptable responses emerging as antidotes to global challenges.

The Role of Technology in Addressing Educational Disparities:

Technology emerges as a catalyzing force in responding to educational disparities. Through the digital prism, we explore how technology is revolutionizing access to education. From virtual classrooms to interactive learning platforms, we see how technology can break down geographical and socio-economic barriers, bringing education to anyone, anywhere. However, it's not just a matter of access; we also examine how technology can enhance the quality of learning, adapting to individual needs and creating a more inclusive educational experience.

The sixth chapter is a profound journey through the intricate terrain of global education challenges, revealing the dark yet surmountable side of our quest for knowledge. From understanding the criticalities to innovative solutions, we prepare to confront the present to build a future where education is truly a universal right.

Chapter 7: "Education for a Sustainable Future"

Importance of Environmental Education:

In the seventh chapter of our journey, we delve into the criticality of environmental education, recognizing that our planet is undergoing an era of unprecedented challenges. The environment, the beating heart of our lives, becomes the central focus. We explore how environmental education goes beyond the concept of "saving the planet," pushing to understand the profound connection between humanity and our environment. Through classrooms and beyond, we seek to cultivate an awareness that sees our destiny intertwined with that of the natural world.

The Contribution of Education to Global Sustainability:

Education emerges as a beacon of light in the darkness of environmental challenges. In this chapter, we examine how knowledge can guide sustainable actions and impact daily decisions. Education becomes a guide, illuminating the path toward global sustainability. From agricultural practices to consumption choices, environmental awareness becomes a currency in building a world where the balance between humanity and nature is at the core of decisions.

Educational Initiatives to Address Climate Challenges:

Through the pages of this chapter, we immerse ourselves in educational initiatives that directly confront climate challenges. From awareness campaigns in schools to the creation of academic programs centered on sustainability, we examine how education can become an agent of change in combating climate change. We observe how teachers and students unite as guardians of our planet, adopting innovative solutions and promoting behaviors that can protect and preserve the fragile beauty of our world.

The seventh chapter of "EnlightenMinds" guides us through the illuminated path of education for a sustainable future. Environmental education is not just a matter of information but of transformation. We flip through the pages of initiatives undertaken by those who recognize the urgency of climate challenges, preparing for a future where education is the key to conserving our planet and channeling human energies toward a sustainable destiny.

Chapter 8: "Future Education: Technology and Creativity"

The Evolution of Education through Technology:

The eighth chapter catapults us into the era of technological revolution, where education unfolds as a playground for innovation. We examine with curious eyes the evolution of learning through technology, from a perspective that goes beyond the mere use of digital tools. From the boom of virtual classrooms to interactive devices, we scrutinize how technology has fused with education, transforming not only the "how" but also the "what" we learn.

*Innovative Approaches to
Teaching:*

The chapter goes beyond
hardware and software, exploring
innovative approaches to
teaching that emphasize the
importance of the learning
experience. From game-based
learning methodologies to
personalized teaching through
artificial intelligence, we witness a
metamorphosis of classrooms
into creative laboratories. With
innovation as our guide, we delve
into educational practices that
challenge conventions, shaping
an environment where every
student can flourish.

*The Role of Creativity in 21st-
Century Education:*

Creativity becomes the keystone
in 21st-century education. In this
chapter, we delve into the central
role of creativity in shaping agile
minds ready to face the
challenges of the future. From

fostering curiosity to encouraging creative problem-solving, education becomes a dance of ideas and expressions. Through projects, collaborations, and stimuli to the imagination, we see how creativity is the driving force behind the formation of global citizens ready to leave a meaningful impact.

Chapter eight of "EnlightenMinds: Journey into the Importance of Education" guides us through the fascinating lands of future education. With technology as a travel companion and creativity as a compass, we discover how learning is transforming into a dynamic experience, shaped by the connection between knowledge and innovation. It is an invitation to imagine a world where education is not just an acquisition of facts but an endless adventure of discovery and creation.

Chapter 9: "Education as a Cultural Bridge"

Education as a Tool for Intercultural Understanding:

The ninth chapter of our journey leads us across a luminous bridge connecting the cultures of the world. Education becomes the connective tissue that unites people of diverse origins and traditions. We explore how learning can overcome linguistic and cultural barriers, opening doors to a deep and respectful understanding of global diversities. Each classroom becomes a crossroads of experiences, transforming education into a powerful means to build bridges of dialogue and mutual understanding.

Educational Programs to Promote Diversity:

Through the pages of this chapter, we discover educational programs actively committed to promoting diversity and inclusion. From initiatives celebrating cultural festivities to exchange programs transporting students to unfamiliar lands, we witness a symphony of educational experiences flourishing in multicultural environments. These programs not only teach facts but shape open minds and tolerant hearts, creating global citizens ready to contribute to global dialogue.

The Role of Education in Overcoming Stereotypes and Prejudices:

The chapter addresses the delicate theme of stereotypes and prejudices, revealing how education stands as a trailblazer in the fight against these obstacles. Through storytelling and concrete examples, we explore how learning can challenge misconceptions and break down walls built on preconceived ideas. Education thus becomes a catalytic force for a society that embraces diversity as richness, not division.

Chapter nine of "EnlightenMinds: Journey into the Importance of Education" guides us through the fertile lands of education as a cultural bridge. In a world that is increasingly interconnected through global ties, we see how learning can become a beacon that illuminates the diversities enriching the human mosaic. With culture as the currency, education becomes a vehicle to build bridges, create bonds, and shape a new generation of global citizens ready to challenge division and embrace unity in diversity.

Chapter 10: "Reflections and Future Challenges"

Assessment of the Evolution of Education:

The final chapter of "EnlightenMinds" invites us on an introspective journey through the evolution of education. We reflect on the paths taken, from ancient classrooms to virtual ones, scrutinizing humanity's journey in its unceasing quest for knowledge. Through the stories of those who have traversed this path, celebrating successes and learning from challenges, we cast a retrospective gaze that offers perspectives for the future.

Future Challenges and How to Address Them:

Looking ahead, aware of the challenges awaiting the future of education. From access to equity, from innovation to sustainability, we acknowledge that the educational journey is a dynamic path that requires constant commitment. In this chapter, we critically examine the challenges on the horizon, outlining strategies and approaches to overcome them. The challenge is not only to adapt to change but to lead change itself, embracing the transformative power of education.

Call to Action: Commitment to a More Educated and Aware World:

Reflection transforms into action as we embark on the final stretch of our journey. With a clear awareness of challenges and opportunities, this chapter concludes with a vibrant call to action. We encourage not only recognizing the importance of education but also being proactive actors in adapting and transforming its future. Every individual, every community, is called upon to contribute to building a more educated, inclusive, and aware world.

The tenth and final chapter of "EnlightenMinds: Journey into the Importance of Education" is an invitation to look to the past, confront the present, and embrace the future with renewed fervor. Through reflections, analysis of future challenges, and a clear call to action, we close this volume with the awareness that education is the most powerful lever to shape the destiny of humanity. We are all protagonists in this ever-evolving story, with the power and duty to illuminate the path for generations to come.

Epilogue: "Towards a Bright Future"

With hearts filled with knowledge and minds ready for new discoveries, we reach the end of "EnlightenMinds: Journey into the Importance of Education." Through centuries of history, we have explored the transformative power of education, illuminating unexplored paths and opening doors to an even brighter future. Every page of this book has been an invitation to consider education not only as a means of learning but as the guiding beacon of our individual and collective evolution.

Our journey has traversed epochs and continents, witnessing education as a social catalyst, an economic engine, and a cultural bridge. We have scrutinized the past, faced the challenges of the present, and cast a bold gaze toward a future where education is the cornerstone of a conscious and sustainable society. Each chapter has been a crucial stop in this endless journey, a story of learning, growth, and hope.

As we close this book, we carry with us the inspiration of those who have made knowledge a driving force for change. We are called to be active protagonists in this narrative, agents of transformation who see education as the vehicle for a fair, equitable, and informed world. Each of us is a precious link in the chain of knowledge, and our commitment to education is an investment in a future that continues to bear fruit.

Appendix: Useful Resources

Educational Organizations:

- UNESCO - United Nations Educational, Scientific and Cultural Organization: https://en.unesco.org/

- World Bank Education: https://www.worldbank.org/en/topic/education

- Education International: https://www.ei-ie.org/

Online Learning Platforms:

- Coursera: https://www.coursera.org/

- edX: https://www.edx.org/

- Khan Academy: https://www.khanacademy.org/

Environmental Education Resources:

- National Geographic Education: https://www.nationalgeographic.org/education/

- Green Education Foundation: http://

*Initiatives for Diversity and
Inclusion:*

- Teaching Tolerance:
  https://www.tolerance.org/

- UNESCO MGIEP -
  Mahatma Gandhi Institute
  of Education for Peace and
  Sustainable Development:
  https://mgiep.unesco.org/

These resources provide a
starting point for those wishing to
delve further into education and
related topics. May each of us
continue to explore, learn, and
contribute to making the world a
better place through the
transformative power of
education.